Morgan Freeman

Julia Holt

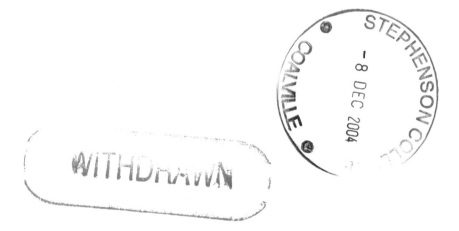

Published in association with The Basic Skills Agency

Hodder & Stoughton

A MEMBER OF THE HODDER HEADLINE GROUP

Acknowledgements

Cover: © E Robert/Corbis Sygma

Photos: © p 3 Popperfoto; pp 5, 9, 13, 15, 17, 22, 28 © Cinetext/Allstar

Every effort has been made to trace copyright holders of material reproduced in this book. Any rights not acknowledged will be acknowledged in subsequent printings if notice is given to the publisher.

Orders; please contact Bookpoint Ltd, 39 Milton Park, Abingdon, Oxon OX14 4TD. Telephone: (44) 01235 400414, Fax: (44) 01235 400454. Lines are open from 9.00–6.00, Monday to Saturday, with a 24 hour message answering service.
Email address: orders@bookpoint.co.uk

British Library Cataloguing in Publication Data
A catalogue record for this title is available from the British Library

ISBN 0 340 77669 2

First published 2000
Impression number   10 9 8 7 6 5 4 3 2 1
Year   2005 2004 2003 2002 2001 2000

Copyright © 2000 Julia Holt

Typeset by GreenGate Publishing Services, Tonbridge, Kent.
Printed in Great Britain for Hodder and Stoughton Educational, a division of Hodder Headline Plc, 338 Euston Road, London NW1 3BH, by Redwood Books, Trowbridge, Wilts

Contents

1 Introduction

There are not many black actors
who have star status in Hollywood.
Most of them still play 'black' parts.
Morgan Freeman does not.
He is cast as an actor,
not as a black actor.

He is also one of the few actors
who can play people twenty years younger
or twenty years older
than his own age.
He is in great demand.

2 Growing Up

Morgan Freeman was born on 1 June 1937
in Memphis Tennessee.
He grew up in Mississippi.
When he was a boy
black and white people
didn't mix together
in the southern states.

Black people had separate schools,
separate seats on buses
and separate seats in cinemas.
They were treated
like second class people.

Morgan Freeman grew up in a world where black people were treated like second-class citizens.

As a little boy
Morgan spent his free time at the cinema.
He put down his twelve cents
and went into his dream world.

He saw his first film aged six.
It was *King Kong*.
He spent most of the film
under the seat.
He had bad dreams for many nights
after *King Kong*.

King Kong gave young Morgan bad dreams.

Morgan Freeman was a tall, skinny kid
who loved to pretend.
He loved reading, music and acting.
Anything to help him to dream.

He had his first acting role
when he was eight.
By the time he was twelve
he knew he had talent.

After High School
he chose to follow his father and brother
into the Air Force.

3 Trying to be an Actor

Morgan wanted to be a jet pilot.
But that was a romantic dream.
Aged seventeen and 6'2" tall,
he became a radar mechanic.

It was not a romantic life at all.
He lasted 3 years, 8 months and 10 days.
In 1959 he got out of the Air Force.
He went to Los Angeles and then to New York
to look for acting work.

There was no acting work for him.
So he took acting classes in an LA college.
Morgan paid for the classes
by working at the same college as a clerk.
When he finished college he went to New York.

In 1964 he married his first wife.
They lived in New York
and he still worked as a clerk.

His take-home pay was $65 a week.
This was not much money
to keep his wife and four children.

Morgan trained as a dancer for five years
but still there was no work.
Then one lunch hour
he raced across the city
to try out as a dancer
for New York's World Fair.
He got the job and never went back
to being a clerk.

Morgan went to New York to try to be an actor.

4 Working in TV

Morgan danced and acted on stage
until 1971, when he got TV work.
It was a children's show
called *The Electric Company*.

He was in the show for five years
but he got very bored.
He was doing something
he didn't want to do.
His career was going nowhere.

His marriage failed and he started drinking.
Morgan says,
'I remember waking up in my doorway,
where I had fallen down.
I lay there thinking, "This will never do".
So I quit drinking.'

He took control of himself.
For the next ten years
he worked on stage, on TV and in films.
But still nothing big came his way.
In 1978 he saw himself on TV for the first time.
He didn't like it and he still doesn't.
He says,
'I don't like looking at me.'

In the early 1980s he nearly gave up
but his second marriage, to Myrna,
gave him hope.

5 The Big Break

Then in 1987,
when Morgan was fifty years old,
he got two big breaks.

The first was a star part
in a film called *Street Smart*.
He played a violent pimp called Fast Black.
The part won him an Oscar nomination.
Morgan liked playing a bad guy.
He's still looking
for another bad guy part to play.

Morgan got his first Oscar nomination for playing Fast Black in *Street Smart*.

The second big break
was in a stage play.
It was called *Driving Miss Daisy*.
It's the story of a rich white woman
and her black driver.
They grow old together and become friends.

Morgan won awards for the stage play.
Then when *Driving Miss Daisy*
was turned into a film in 1989
he was nominated for another Oscar.

Morgan Freeman starred in the film and the play of *Driving Miss Daisy.*

6 Making History

Morgan Freeman is a keen student of history.
He surfs the Internet for information.
He says,
'The future is in the Internet.
How can you not be there?'

In 1989 Morgan was proud
to be in the film *Glory*.
The film is set in the 1860s.
It's the story of the first black unit
from the North,
to fight in the American Civil War.
The film was his chance
to retell history.

Morgan Freeman in *Glory*, a film about the American Civil War.

Morgan chooses films that interest him.
But this doesn't mean
that they are always hits.
He has made films
that didn't make much money.

Robin Hood with Kevin Costner
and *Chain Reaction* with Keanu Reeves
were not big box office hits.
But no-one blames Morgan.
His acting is always worth watching.

7 Morgan's Best Films

Morgan was back with another
Oscar nomination in 1994.
It was for his acting in *The Shawshank Redemption*.
It's the story of a bunch of prisoners,
their time in prison
and how one of them escapes.

A lot of people
put *The Shawshank Redemption*
in their list of top ten films.

The next year
Morgan Freeman was in a blockbuster.

He had a star part in *Seven*.
He played a burnt-out cop
who was hunting a serial killer
with Brad Pitt.
The killer is killing people
to show the seven deadly sins,
like greed and envy.

It was a very dark film
without a happy ending.
Even the air looks gloomy in the film.
They did this
by blowing oil and water into the air.
It gave everyone a bad cough.

In *Seven*, Brad Pitt used method acting
to get into his part.
Method acting is when the actor tries to become
the character they are playing.
Morgan didn't use method acting.
He says,
'There are no tricks.
I just put on the clothes and learn the lines.
I wasn't trained to act.
I was trained to walk, talk and dance.
Nobody teaches you how to act.'

Seven went on to make
more than $100 million.

The film *Seven* was a huge hit.

In 1997 Morgan played another cop
hunting another serial killer.
The film was called *Kiss The Girls*.
People said that it was just another *Seven*
but it wasn't.

This time the cop was flashy.
He drove a Porsche.
His name was Dr Alex Cross
and he was in his forties.
He was not affected by his work
until his niece was taken by a serial killer.

There are many more books about Dr Alex Cross.
So we might see Morgan
playing him again.

After *Kiss The Girls*
Morgan was about to spend the winter sailing.
He has a 38′ sail boat
moored in the Virgin Islands.
He was asked to work on a new film
called *Amistad*.

He couldn't turn it down
because it was another chance
to retell history.
Amistad is the true story
of 53 African slaves.
They were on a ship called the *Amistad*
in 1839.

The Africans didn't want to be slaves.
So they got together
and killed the slavers.
They were put on trial in America
for murder.

Morgan played a freed slave.
He helped the Africans to get a fair trial.
It's a bit of history
that not many people know about.
But they do now, thanks to *Amistad*.

Morgan said,
'People are going to walk away from *Amistad*
thinking differently.'

8 Success at Fifty

Morgan's knack of picking hit films
led him to play the US President
in *Deep Impact* in 1998.
In the film he tells the American people
that there is going to be a lottery
to choose who will hide in caves
to be safe when a meteor
crashes into the Earth.

The film was another smash hit.
It made $40 million in its opening weekend.

Morgan Freeman didn't become a star
until he was fifty.
Now he's a millionaire.
He used to dream about sailing round the world
but he had too much work to do.
So now he says, 'I'm living my big dreams.'

He lives on a 44 acre horse ranch
with Myrna, his wife,
and one of their ten grandchildren.

There are many more films in the pipeline
for Morgan Freeman.
Some of them will be made
by his own film company.
It's called Revelations Entertainment.

One new film is very special.
It's the film of the life of Nelson Mandela.
It tells the story of his life
from being a cow herder
to being South Africa's first black president.

Morgan will play Mandela in later life.
It's another chance for him
to retell history.

Morgan will retell history when he plays Nelson Mandela.